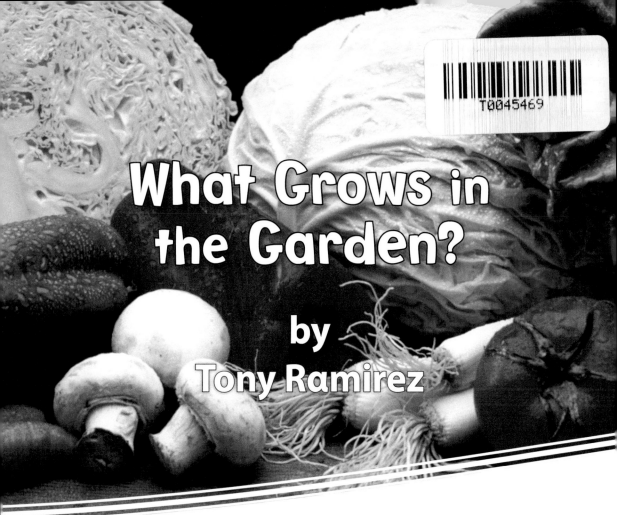

What Grows in the Garden?

by
Tony Ramirez

NATIONAL GEOGRAPHIC

Hampton-Brown

National Geographic and the Yellow Border are registered trademarks of the National Geographic Society.

National Geographic School Publishing
Hampton-Brown
www.NGSP.com

Printed in Mexico

ISBN: 978-0-7362-7989-5

Print Number: 10   Print Year: 2020

Acknowledgments and credits continue on the inside back cover.

This is a tomato.

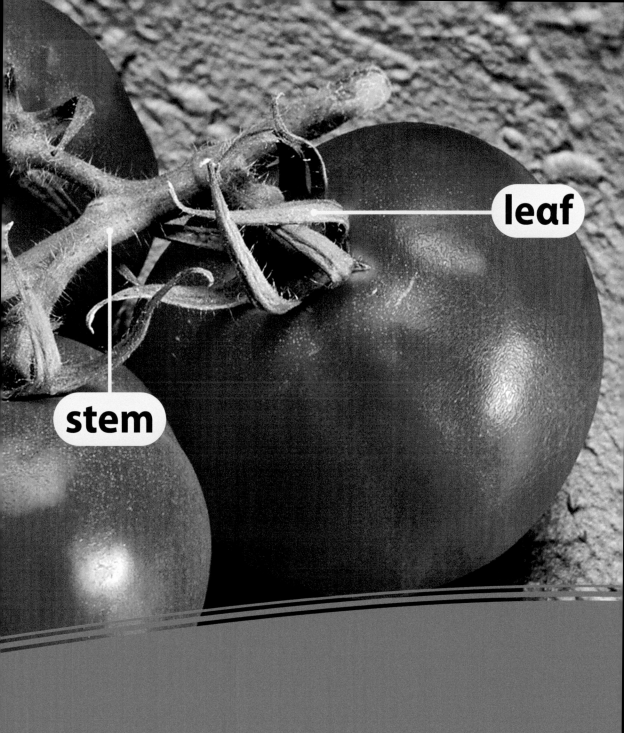

leaf

stem

It has a stem and a leaf.

root

This is a carrot.

It has a leaf and a root.

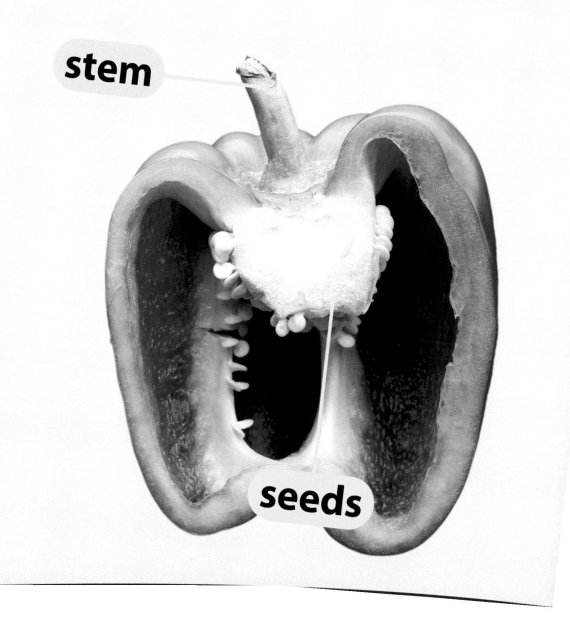

stem

seeds

This is a salad. It has tomatoes, carrots, and peppers!